D0473650

1860

Feel Good

Understand Your Emotions

by Kathy Feeney

Consultant:
Jenifer Wood, Ph.D.
Vice President of Services and Research
National Mental Health Association

Bridgestone Books
an imprint of Capstone Press
Mankato, Minnesota

Bridgestone Books are published by Capstone Press
151 Good Counsel Drive, P.O. Box 669, Mankato, Minnesota 56002
http://www.capstone-press.com

Printed in the United States of America.

Library of Congress Cataloging-in-Publication Data
Feeney, Kathy, 1954–
Feel good: understand your emotions/by Kathy Feeney.
p. cm.—(Your health)
Includes bibliographical references and index (p. 24).
ISBN 0-7368-0972-4
1. Emotions in children—Juvenile literature. [1. Emotions.] I. Title. II. Series.
BF723.E6 F46 2002
152.4—dc21 00-012536

Summary: An introduction to the understanding of emotions, how to share emotions in positive ways, handling disagreements, and the importance of good self-esteem.

Editorial Credits
Sarah Lynn Schuette, editor; Karen Risch, product planning editor; Linda Clavel, designer and illustrator

Photo Credits
Comstock, Inc., cover, 12, 20
David F. Clobes, Stock Photography, 4
Gregg R. Andersen, 6, 10, 14, 16, 18
PhotoDisc, Inc., 8
Rubberball Productions, 1

Bridgestone Books thanks Mari Schuh, Connie Colwell, and Franklin Elementary School, Mankato, Minnesota, for providing photo shoot locations.

1 2 3 4 5 6 07 06 05 04 03 02

Table of Contents

Your Emotions

You show how you feel through your emotions. There are many types of emotions. You can be happy, sad, scared, angry, and jealous. Everyone shows emotions in different ways.

emotion
a strong feeling

Guess What?

Eating healthy food helps your mind and body feel good.

Feeling Happy

Feeling happy is feeling pleased about something. You may smile or laugh when you are happy. You sometimes sing, whistle, or dance to show your happiness. Doing nice things for others helps you feel happy.

Try This!

Watch a funny movie with a friend. It might cheer you up when you feel sad.

Feeling Sad

Everyone feels sad sometimes. Crying is one way to show sadness. Grief is another type of sadness. You may feel grief when someone you know dies.

grief
a feeling of great sadness

Feeling Scared

Feeling scared means being afraid. You feel scared when you do not feel safe. A dark room or basement may scare you. You sometimes can have a stomachache or sweaty hands when you feel scared.

Try This!

Count to ten when you are angry. Think before you say or do something that could hurt others.

Feeling Angry

Everyone feels angry sometimes. Anger is feeling mad about something. You may want to yell, cry, or hit. You sometimes say mean things when you are angry. Angry actions and words can hurt other people.

Try This!

When you feel jealous, make a list of five things that you are thankful for.

Feeling Jealous

Feeling jealous means wanting what others have. You may be jealous of a friend's backpack, toy, or clothes. Jealousy can cause other emotions such as anger or sadness.

Sharing Your Feelings

Sharing your feelings helps you understand your emotions. Talk to someone you trust about your emotions. Try writing your feelings in a journal. Drawing or painting is another way to share your emotions.

journal
a private diary or notebook

Handling Disagreements

Everyone has different emotions and opinions. Sometimes you disagree with someone else. Disagreements can cause anger. Talk about the problem. Listen to each other. You can learn to work together and compromise when you disagree.

compromise
to agree to something that is not exactly what you wanted in order to make a decision

Feeling Good

Sharing your emotions and taking care of your body helps you feel good. Feeling good helps you feel proud of yourself. This is called self-esteem. Help others feel good by treating them with respect.

self-esteem
feelings of pride and respect for yourself

Hands On: Make Someone Laugh

Everybody knows how to laugh. Laughing helps people feel happy. One of the easiest ways to make people laugh is to tell a joke. Here are some elephant jokes to try on your friends and family:

What do you call an elephant that flies?
A jumbo jet!

Why were the elephants thrown out of the swimming pool?
Because they could not hold their trunks up!

What time is it when an elephant sits on a fence?
Time to fix the fence!

Why did the elephant paint her toenails red?
So she could hide in the cherry tree!

What do you get if you cross an elephant with a kangaroo?
Gigantic holes all over Australia!

Try making up your own jokes.

Words to Know

compromise (KOM-pruh-mize)—to agree to something that is not exactly what you wanted in order to make a decision

emotion (e-MOH-shuhn)—a strong feeling; people have and show emotions such as happiness, sadness, fear, anger, and jealousy.

grief (GREEF)—a feeling of great sadness; people usually feel grief when someone they know dies.

opinion (uh-PIN-yuhn)—an idea or belief that people have about something; people have different opinions.

self-esteem (SELF ess-TEEM)—feelings of pride and respect for yourself; people who have self-esteem feel good about themselves.

Read More

Fisher, Enid. *Emotional Ups and Downs.* Good Health Guides. Milwaukee: Gareth Stevens, 1998.

Kent, Susan. *Learning How to Feel Good about Yourself.* The Violence Prevention Library. New York: PowerKids Press, 2001.

Raatma, Lucia. *Respect.* Character Education. Mankato, Minn.: Bridgestone Books, 2000.

Internet Sites

How Do You Feel?
http://www.pbs.org/rogers/make_believe/feel.htm

Talking About Your Feelings
http://kidshealth.org/kid/feeling/thought/talk_feelings.html

Index